I0162778

# Momma Said

A poem of tribute to my wise
Grandmother

By

Alice Curtis

All Scripture references are from the King James Version of The Bible

Cover photo composite: Thompson family/A. Curtis

All rights reserved

Copyright 2018

## Dedication:

Thanks Mom for your encouraging love, thanks to my brother for always pointing to a better day, thanks to my Aunts for all their love and to all my family for sharing their memories so freely, without which none of this remembrance could have been put to paper.

Plus, a special thank you to all Mothers who "speak the truth in love."

Thy word is a lamp unto my feet, and a light unto my path.

Psalm 119:105

Lying securely on my comfy bed

I remember things my Momma said.

Words of instruction sprinkled with love

Inspired by wisdom from the **LORD** above.

I can do all things through Christ which strengtheneth me.

Philippians 4:13

On days when life was
filled with dread

How it helped to
remember what dear
Momma said.

When defeat, in my life,
clouded my day

Momma said, "Where
there's a will there's a
way."

For the Lord GOD will help me; therefore shall I not be confounded: therefore have I set my face like a flint, and I know that I shall not be ashamed.

Isaiah 50:7

Our lives were sometimes fraught with disappointments and pain

But the words of blessing she gave us, in our hearts remain.

She never let us give up our dreams or live with regret.

Momma said, "Don't you say can't,

Say you ain't yet!"

The righteous eateth to the satisfying of his soul: but the belly of the wicked shall want.

Proverbs 13:25

Or when thoughts of
doubt filled my head

I would remember what
sweet Momma said.

When empty cupboard
doors opened with a
hollow swing

"With flour and milk
and sugar you can make
anything."

Two are better than one; because they have a good reward for their labour. For if they fall, the one will lift up his fellow: but woe to him that is alone when he falleth; for he hath not another to help him up. And if one prevail against him, two shall withstand him; and a threefold cord is not quickly broken.

Ecclesiastes 4:9-10 and 12

Discouragement weighing my feet down like lead

Brought to mind more words dear Momma said.

To us siblings when chores outlasted the setting sun

"Work together and you can get it done."

He that keepeth his mouth keepeth his life: but he that openeth wide his lips shall have destruction.

Proverbs 13:3

Mom never said
anything bad about
anyone
And that's what she
taught us till the day
was done.
"If you can't say
something nice then
don't say anything at
all."
With her sage words, we
learned with humility to
stand tall.

Dearly beloved, avenge not yourselves, but rather give place unto wrath: for it is written, Vengeance is mine; I will repay, saith the Lord.

Romans 12:19

Injustice prompting
anger that would
threaten to overcome
the day
Brought forth more
words my Momma did
say.
Made us give up the
resentful answer that it
was...
"You need your nose as
much as your face
does."

These six things doth the LORD hate: yea, seven are an abomination unto him: A proud look, a lying tongue, and hands that shed innocent blood, An heart that deviseth wicked imaginations, feet that be swift in running to mischief, A false witness that speaketh lies, and he that soweth discord among brethren.

Proverbs 6:16-19

Or when the sin of pride reared its ugly head

I remember her response, what Momma said.

"Anybody that's right all the time is wrong in the first place."

Words for all drawing breath, every color and every race.

The meek shall eat and be satisfied: they shall praise the LORD that seek him: your heart shall live for ever.

Psalm 22:26

"If you're full it don't matter what you ate."

Her oh so true words you could not escape.

Whether a plate of fruit or greens or meat

We learned with gratitude to go off to sleep.

Come, eat of my bread, and drink of the wine which I have mingled.  Forsake the foolish, and live; and go in the way of understanding.

Proverbs 9:5-6

When childish and immature we would be

I can remember what she said to help us see.

Without malice and without pretense

Momma said, "That don't make a lick of sense!"

Ponder the path of thy feet, and let all thy ways be established.

Proverbs 4:26

Her words could make you, in your tracks, stop dead.

A prudent warning is what Momma said.

"If you knew what walked the streets at night you wouldn't go out."

Truth again uttered without a doubt.

He becometh poor that dealeth with a slack hand: but the hand of the diligent maketh rich.

Proverbs 10:4

We'd walk through the town past those with more than we had.

How I needed to hear the words Momma said.

Encouraging as always, bringing hope when envy made us sad.

"These are the kinds of places that you can all have!"

Then Peter opened his mouth, and said, Of a truth I perceive that God is no respecter of persons: But in every nation he that feareth him, and worketh righteousness, is accepted with him.

Acts 10:34-35

Words to help build
character echo as a
poetic refrain.
If you lay quietly you
can hear Momma's
words again.
"There's nobody better
than you and you're no
better than anybody
else."
With every intonation
her teachings gave
needed help.

Honour thy father and mother; which is the first commandment with promise; That it may be well with thee, and thou mayest live long on the earth.

Ephesians 6:2-3

And when as a child I
honored not my Dad

It was foolish to resist
what my Momma said.

The truth was that what
she said to daughters
and sons

She was right when told,
"But he's your Father,
hon."

A fool's wrath is presently known: but a prudent man covereth shame.

Proverbs 12:16

Or when something
would get us mad as sin

From her lips came
words worthy of
absorbing in.

Simple words of gentle
admonition from her
lips escaped

Momma said, "You're
bent out of shape."

The hearing ear, and the seeing eye, the LORD hath made
even both of them.
Proverbs 20:12

It is of the LORD's mercies that we are not consumed,
because his compassions fail not. They are new every
morning: great is thy faithfulness.
Lamentations 3:22-23

Train up a child in the way he should go: and when he is old,
he will not depart from it.
Proverbs 22:6

When schoolwork confused, "What do you see?"
When a day was filled with trouble, "It'll be better in the morning. Try to go to sleep."
When children's needs overwhelm, "Children have the first thing in your life."
So we wouldn't be "out done," giving us tools to work thru life's strife.

Be thou diligent to know the state of thy flocks, and look
well to thy herds.

Proverbs 27:23

Pray without ceasing.

1 Thessalonians 5:17

Simple help when what little we had was almost not…

"You have to take care of what you got."

Saying "Most people pray when they sit down to eat.

I pray before I go into the kitchen." Her faith-filled words so soft and sweet.

Hope deferred maketh the heart sick: but when the desire cometh, it is a tree of life.

Proverbs 13:12

And when the responsibility of family came after being wed

Can't help remembering what our own Momma said.

"You have to do for a child when he needs it hon."

So determine to do the best for them no matter what must be done.

For God so loved the world, that he gave his only begotten Son, that whosoever believeth in him should not perish, but have everlasting life.

John 3:16

"Tell children about Christ. All children should go to church." Her 6th grade educated fingers wrote.

"Please carry your children to church so they can learn of the Bible," said her note.

"Christmas means Christ; love is why we give presents," she taught us of God's greatest gift in Jesus His Son.

And Momma said what her heart knew from Him as she loved us every one.

Lo, children are an heritage of the LORD: and the fruit of the womb is his reward.

Psalm 127:3

When some found she
endured 11 pregnancies
in her day;

"I didn't have a single
one I could have done
without," I can still hear
her say.

All of her children were
cherished, each and
every one.

And she loved them
with all her strength,
every daughter and
every son.

The hoary head is a crown of glory, if it be found in the way of righteousness.

Proverbs 16:31

Later in life she was asked about getting old

Her words again brought forth wisdom of gold.

With gratitude to the LORD she cheerfully conceded,

Momma said, "There was something in every year that was needed."

Keep thy tongue from evil, and thy lips from speaking guile.

Psalm 34:13

When things were going
not like they ought to
have been
She shook her head and
from the frustration
away she'd bend.
Set always to keep her
tongue kind and guile-
free
She'd sigh deeply and
say in exasperation, "O
I swannee!"

THE LORD is my shepherd; I shall not want. He maketh me to lie down in green pastures: he leadeth me beside the still waters. He restoreth my soul: he leadeth me in the paths of righteousness for his name's sake.

Psalm 23:1-3

After a long life of
service, fatigue
weighing down like lead
Quiet confessions, that
our undaunted but not
as strong, Momma said.
Resting for just a
moment so once again
she could arise,
"Oh no hon, I'm not
sleeping. I'm just
resting my eyes."

Happy is the man that findeth wisdom, and the man that getteth understanding. For the merchandise of it is better than the merchandise of silver, and the gain thereof than fine gold. She is more precious than rubies: and all the things thou canst desire are not to be compared unto her.

Proverbs 3:13-15

Momma encouraged us in ways only a Mother could

For she always, in the bad, found the good.

Wisdom through her words like a golden thread,

These are the things our noble and kind Momma said.

www.ingramcontent.com/pod-product-compliance
Lightning Source LLC
Chambersburg PA
CBHW060621030426
42337CB00018B/3134